Ravenous Words

Praise for *Ravenous Words*

"'But let's be real,' the poet wrote. And indeed these are poems that tell the truth and are nothing if not real. *Ravenous Words*, a courageous collaboration of poetic worlds, are Sue's memories and Lisa's portraits, Sue's defiance and Lisa's unsentimental observations. Listening to their poems converse among themselves, through the synergy of their nightmares and daydreams juxtaposed and woven together, we hear, among the voices of spirit animals and endangered seals, of silent monks and plucky travelers, the words of 'girls who know how to fight.'"

—Janet N. Gold, Professor Emerita, Languages,
Literatures and Cultures, University of New Hampshire

"Follow the currents of this shared conversation between two very different poets and come away with a unique sense of what it means to collaborate. These often hard-earned poems of experience—deeply female, familial, environmental, and lyrical—bring their themes to shore in one urgent song, a kind of pact in verse that commands our attention."

—Kate Sontag, co-editor of *After Confession:
Poetry as Autobiography*, (Graywolf)

"With ravenous passions spanning personal and family history, geography, nature, food, and current events (addressing a range of issues including the pandemic, racism, migrant workers, and sexual assault), poets Wurtzburg and Lucas have imparted to their readers a 'quilted heritage' of experience and image in which 'the world folds, like a handkerchief, and we balance on its crease.'"

—Pamela Wax, author of
Walking the Labyrinth (Main Street Rag, 2022)
and *Starter Mothers* (Finishing Line Press, 2023)

Ravenous Words

SUSAN J. WURTZBURG   LISA LUCAS

Brandylane
Publishers, Inc.
Publishing books since 1985

Cover Image:
Huginn & Muninn (mind and memory)
2022 by James Lahey
© James Lahey Studio

Copyright © 2025 by Susan J. Wurtzburg and Lisa Lucas

All rights reserved. No part of this book may be reproduced in any form or by any electronic or mechanical means, or the facilitation thereof, including information storage and retrieval systems, without permission in writing from the publisher, except in the case of brief quotations published in articles and reviews. Any educational institution wishing to photocopy part or all of the work for classroom use, or individual researchers who would like to obtain permission to reprint the work for educational purposes, should contact the publisher.

ISBN (Paperback): 978-1-962416-98-6
ISBN (Hardcover): 978-1-962416-97-9
Library of Congress Control Number: 2025902493

Designed by Sami Langston
Project managed by Andrew Holt

Published by
Brandylane Publishers, Inc.
5 S. 1st Street
Richmond, Virginia 23219

brandylanepublishers.com

For Christopher, Diana, Zoë, and Virginia

Photo by Charlie Lehoczky

Contents

"And once sent out a word takes wing" (Horace) 1
A Murder of Crows 3
    Susan J. Wurtzburg
Memory and Thought 4
    Lisa Lucas

"The raven gave a short . . . croak" (Charles Dickens) 5
Old Mirror 6
    Lisa Lucas
Out of the Box in the USA 7
    Susan J. Wurtzburg
Final Passage 8
    Susan J. Wurtzburg
Dancing Eyes 9
    Lisa Lucas
Pink Steel Rocket 10
    Lisa Lucas

"These wisest men" (Friedrich Nietzsche) 12
Why Indeed? 13
    Susan J. Wurtzburg
Blue-lit Coyotes 14
    Lisa Lucas
Pegasus Defeats a Bullet 15
    Susan J. Wurtzburg
Visceral Words 16
    Lisa Lucas
Endangered Hawaii 17
    Susan J. Wurtzburg
Stuck 18
    Lisa Lucas
Sliding over the Edge 19
    Susan J. Wurtzburg
Blue Smoke 20
    Lisa Lucas
The Barn Reapers 21
    Susan J. Wurtzburg
Tomato Fingers 22
    Lisa Lucas
Journey to Mitnal 23
    Susan J. Wurtzburg
There Be Dragons 24
    Susan J. Wurtzburg

Transformation 25
    Susan J. Wurtzburg

"We saw a raven" (Dorothy Wordsworth) 26
The Howl and Silence... 27
    Lisa Lucas
Ocean Alchemy.. 28
    Susan J. Wurtzburg
Sounds... 29
    Lisa Lucas
Grave Distance.. 30
    Susan J. Wurtzburg
Family Skeletons... 31
    Susan J. Wurtzburg
Open to the Void.. 32
    Susan J. Wurtzburg
Beached... 33
    Susan J. Wurtzburg

"He flies for the joy of flying" (Virginia Moore) 34
Old Monk 35
    Lisa Lucas
My Friend Said.. 36
    Susan J. Wurtzburg
Winter Light.. 37
    Lisa Lucas
Midnight Stallions.. 38
    Susan J. Wurtzburg

"Under wide driven wings" (Glenn Ward Dresbach) 39
Daffodils 40
    Susan J. Wurtzburg
Here's the thing 41
    Lisa Lucas
We Call This Land 42
    Susan J. Wurtzburg
The Damn Page.. 43
    Lisa Lucas
A Very British War 45
    Susan J. Wurtzburg
Bumper Cars and Rockets.. 46
    Lisa Lucas
Quilted Heritage 47
    Susan J. Wurtzburg

Loot, Bookmarks, and The J Stroke 48
    Lisa Lucas
Departures 49
    Susan J. Wurtzburg
In the Mountains 50
    Susan J. Wurtzburg
Inside 51
    Lisa Lucas

"What are these ravens doing?" (Louis Untermeyer) 53
A Louisiana Rabbit 54
    Susan J. Wurtzburg
Caste Wars 55
    Lisa Lucas
Almost Airborne 57
    Susan J. Wurtzburg
His Mother's Words 58
    Lisa Lucas
Identity Bracelets 60
    Susan J. Wurtzburg
Self Portrait 61
    Lisa Lucas
Travels with My Brother 62
    Susan J. Wurtzburg
The Attraction of Grief 64
    Lisa Lucas
If You Can 65
    Lisa Lucas
I've Seen Everything (Case #08-28) 66
    Lisa Lucas

"O sweet and luminous Bird" (Jessica Powers) 68
My Sister 69
    Susan J. Wurtzburg
Two Meals 70
    Lisa Lucas
Narnia Notions 71
    Susan J. Wurtzburg
Her North Star 72
    Lisa Lucas
Pandemic Journeys 73
    Susan J. Wurtzburg
Her Spirit Animal 74
    Lisa Lucas

Eating the Rainbow 75
    Susan J. Wurtzburg
Rectangular Treasure 76
    Lisa Lucas
Sweet with a Dash of Salt 77
    Susan J. Wurtzburg
Disconnected 78
    Lisa Lucas

Credits 79
About the Authors 81

Acknowledgements

I so appreciate the colleagues and friends who provided helpful edits on these poems. I would especially like to call out the members of the Poetry Writing Shared Interest Group at the Osher Lifelong Learning Institute (OLLI) at Berkshire Community College, the participants in the *Rat's Ass Review* Online Poetry Workshop, and the members of the Red Butte Bards Chapter of the League of Utah Writers. Special thanks are due to Kate Sontag, who ran several poetry classes that helped me build my writing skills. Plus, I am most grateful for the many months of editing with my co-author, Lisa, who is a poetry collaborator par-excellence.

—Susan J. Wurtzburg

I've heard that very few people care about poetry until they need it. They need to make sense of something that has happened. Well, I guess I must have really needed it because I'm completely hooked. It was my good fortune to work with Susan on this project. She taught me that poetry allows a writer freedom. She once compared it to modern art - a canvas waiting for expression with few or even no rules. I found that the hardest part. The idea of no guardrails often sent me to the moon. But luckily, Susan would always take the time to quietly suggest, gently steer or simply say, "Lisa, you can do better than that." We all know that only the best mentors do that. Thank you Sue.

—Lisa Lucas

"And once sent out a word takes wing beyond recall."

Horace (65-8 BC) *Epistles*

A Murder of Crows
Susan J. Wurtzburg

Crows commit murder in red pines above the roof,
c-c-c-caws slice silent air inside. If thoughts carried knives,
we would all be red pierced, instead, bloodshot eyes.

Lips quiver, I swallow my sounds, bury them deep
into my chest. Blue eyes blink, look at my father,
summons to eat food prepared by mute mother.

Barbequed meat on the table, blackened crust,
rosy inside, view of a fragmented heart. Broken,
I flee the anger and alcohol, words unspoken.

Once again, dampen the hay stalks with tears, alone
in the ponded field. Eventually, struggle up the slope;
after all, only fourteen, and I still have much hope.

Memory and Thought
Lisa Lucas

Odin, you Viking King,
all powerful, a true visionary,
sitting erect on your throne with your long beard and single eye.

You were so brave to sacrifice the other,
fill the deep black socket with wisdom.

What a daunting move!

Odin, how is it that you always look so virile on that eight-legged horse
with your long hair flowing behind?
You must know it makes for a dashing sight—and that knife
tucked in your belt, poised and perfect for battle,
do you sharpen it yourself?

Everyone knows you're the Master of Words,
the way you play with them,
tweak them to become lethal weapons.

Odin, please tell me all about your two faithful ravens:
Huginn and Muninn.
Did you really tell them to fly around the world to gather information?

I've heard that on their return, you ordered them
to open their thick black beaks, and a gush of twisted information flowed out
full of hate and loathing . . .

        caw

              caw

                    caw

and with each hoarse, raucous sound
you planned every kill you could possibly make.

Oh, you wise Viking God!

"The raven gave a short, comfortable, confidential kind of croak; — a most expressive croak, which seemed to say, 'You needn't let these fellows into our secrets. We understand each other. It's all right.'"

Charles Dickens (1841) *Barnaby Ridge*

Old Mirror
Lisa Lucas

Her eyes sparkle just before she nails
her jokes
her words
clever
funny
mostly dry.

Listen
really listen
'cause one might whiz by whoooooshhhhhhhh like a gust of wind
and the smiles
the laughter
lost.

Lately her eyes
dart back and forth
an old mirror warps her words

    sTill cleVer, sTill dRy

but now reflects
the residue
of disappointments.

Out of the Box in the USA
Susan J. Wurtzburg

Headline: "Crayola launches box of crayons
with diverse skin tones,"
—positive step in a dumpster fire.
Will knowing that children colour their stick figures
Light Almond or *Extra Deep Golden*
keep me from despair?
Partial to drawings of purple-tinted mothers
with green spiky hair, fathers with deliciously blue skin,
cranberry locks.
Families of brilliantly coloured shapes,
oddly sized figures, floating under yellow suns,
with dragons in the sky—

Crayola markets "Colours of the World,"
so well intentioned, somewhat like pageant winners
mumbling "world peace."
Will it mean anything to an incarcerated young Black father
that his child sends him drawings
toned accurately?
Will it be helpful to a Black mother, whose sister died
in childbirth, that her niece
draws her skin *Deep Golden*?
Will voting disenfranchisement of entire communities
be changed by
Very Deep Rose pencils?

Baby steps to wholehearted,
comprehensive change.
Colour me *Light Medium Almond*.

Final Passage
Susan J. Wurtzburg

He died today, a passing of dragons and rainbows.
Wouldn't we all like to exit in a mixture of sun and rain?
Rise high in the sky, dream weather turbulence. Flight
of his consciousness from the white-walled hospital room.
Eyes shut, heart beats, an almost-abandoned body waits
for departure, frail figure lost in a blue-patterned gown.

Man in the afternoon rainbow, with awareness left behind
in orange, clotted like thick cream. Between yellow and green,
lips turn indigo. No words left, just a rattle with a plunge
into the dragon's maw. Fire-forged breath marks the sunset.
Dusk's curtain falls, stars rise, no change to the constellations.

But oh,
    for this daughter,
        the world darkens with his passage.

Dancing Eyes
Lisa Lucas

She's a lot older than me,
seems younger.

Her eyes
always dancing,
wild,
a bit scary.

When a smile emerges,
broad and beautiful,
and her voice lifts,

> *You know, you'd be good at that!*

I laugh inside.

What is she thinking?

I could never do that.

In my aloneness,
her words,
safe and cocooned,
give me the strength
to do just the thing
I could never.

And when I tell her
she's the reason,
her eyes take a bow,

> *Oh yes, I did say that!*

(For Robin)

Pink Steel Rocket
Lisa Lucas

Bella agreed to drive her.

Reluctantly.

She waited in the driver's seat,
sweltering, with the door open,
her pores oozing moisture and oil.

With bare thighs plastered to the seat,
a putrid smell surged in her nostrils.

She grabbed the keys to start the engine,
with sweaty fingers
and desperate fumbling,
the AC finally blew, and sweet relief followed.

Until Zoey strutted out,
wrapped tightly in a camel coat,
brown wool-lined boots hugging her legs,
leather gloves pulled high,
a thick wool tam yanked down,
and a soft mohair scarf encompassing the rest
so that only her eyes peeped out
for limited view.

For a moment, Bella imagined Zoey as an astronaut,
strapped in a pink steel rocket,
protected . . .

The image burst when Zoey snuggled herself into the passenger seat,
flicked off the AC,
flung open the door,
inhaled a long, deep breath,
her lungs only satisfied
once replete with hot, dense air.

And while Bella burned hotter,
nauseated with acid welling up in her throat,

Zoey sang,

Heat Waves,
You can't fight it,
You can't breathe . . .

without a bead of sweat
or whisper of discomfort,
tucked under her soft mohair scarf,
happily encapsulated.

"These wisest men of all ages should be scrutinized closely. Were they all perhaps shaky on their legs? Tottery? Decadent? Late? Could it be that wisdom appears on earth as a Raven, attracted by a little whiff of carrion?"

Friedrich Nietzsche (1889) *Twilight of the Idols*

Why Indeed?
Susan J. Wurtzburg

When I was a teen, I noticed—too often imprinted
    on my firm skin—men's hands.
Five spread, sausage-like appendages, connected
    by a sweaty palm pressed to my body.

I apparently was just a set of buttocks
    walking down the street, a pluckable apple.
Hungry males felt no need to ask permission;
    seemed I didn't own the tree or the orchard.

Pickable ripeness available to any outstretched hand
    while working, subway riding, or running.
Exploring a public street, I learned that my body
    could be tossed to the ground and peeled.

A defiant core pinned to earth, yelling
    at those nearby,
        help me,
            please help.

Aid never given, always self-rescued,
    heroine of my stories, yes, stories.

Accounts like these don't stop people asking,
"why didn't she just report it?"

        Why indeed,
            why indeed?

Blue-lit Coyotes
Lisa Lucas

. . . midnight
bedroom still

a full moon invades the space
casts blue-lit shadows of coyotes that roam the floor

adrenaline rushes
clenches the heart
overrides the mind
smacks the face

time to move
walk it out
drink water
stop the buzz
until the door opens and the coyotes shrink . . .

weak and weary

climb into bed

it's over
for now

Pegasus Defeats a Bullet
Susan J. Wurtzburg

Prisoner in the passenger seat of a truck, body shiver. Pale
fingers, clammy-clasped in my lap, shake. His hands control
the wheel, and life, a firearm within reach. Another weapon,
this man's desire, about which I have no illusions. His deceptive plan
a brutal sexual assault, but then what? I fear a quiet bush burial.

My only advantages: calm exterior, knowledge of the terrain.
    When he veers off the road to Belmopan, I know it will be soon.

Without warning,
    fling open the door,
        throw myself to the gravel.

My shirt rips as he grabs,
    but fails to stop my full-body plunge.

A quick twist sideways,
    as a grooved tire twitches dust by my head.

Skid screeches,
    dark gun-mouth points my way, entry to the grave.

I beg, tears drip off my chin. Eyes upon him, plea to stop the bullets.
I back down the dusty jungle road, then turn into a jagged run.
Hooves and a saviour's voice echoes, roar from aloft, man on a horse.
Pegasus, a black giant mounted on a nag rescues a small white girl.

Visceral Words
Lisa Lucas

She loved her words,
always controlled when she spoke,
concise when she wrote,
a wordsmith of sorts.

The day the puppy arrived,
the seven-pound furball with the pure heart,
her words grew more precise,
each one a calculation.

But when a three-legged monster attacked
and she spotted a man leaning on a post,
a slight smirk emerging,
her words exploded into an unconscious burst,

    GET YOUR FUCKING DOG OFF MINE!

Later, after the surgeries,
stitches removed and scars faded,
she reminisced about how *good*
she felt that day.

Endangered Hawaii
Susan J. Wurtzburg

Kaiwi drops a male at Kaimana Beach. Hawaii Monk Seal
pup, teeny-tiny adorable, plump sausage, lash-framed eyes.
Image bounces across Oahu: media-birthed celebrity.
Optimism for this baby and his fourteen hundred endangered furry kin,
delight in the moment, as a small plastic bag blows by.

Excited tourists and locals peer through orange barriers,
push cameras through gaps, frame their lives in sunny shots.
Brief focus on marine wildlife, next an introduced parrot
in a palm, finally a blue Hawaiian cocktail on the beach,
shift to relaxation as a small plastic bag blows by.

Miles from Waikiki, another seal hauls up on the beach,
fishing filament decorates his neck, enwraps bloodied muzzle,
plastic drips on a flipper, medallion on a full-body necklace.
His beauty unremarked, no one there to remove his jewelry,
a corpse-in-waiting bakes as a small plastic bag blows by . . .

Stuck
Lisa Lucas

She hangs on the bedroom screen
slams her wings to the metal
caught in the sharp minuscule squares

frantic
she arches her back
expands her wings
a cascade of colour bursts
until her legs twist
rendering her immoveable

cutting metal
subdues

her will
her strength
her freedom.

Sliding over the Edge
Susan J. Wurtzburg

The Yokohama coast where railway tracks hold the land
    close to the seashore like a giant zipper.
Wooden sleepers stretch north to Kaena Point,
    an albatross sanctuary on Oahu's rocky tip.

A promontory across the ocean, and many mountain ranges
    from my father, lost to geography.

The landscape impinges on his daylight hours:
    four white walls, a wheelchair, and a door.
No entrance to the world. He has exited his mind,
    and left his body, an empty shell.

This dry husk of a man, confined to a bed, no walking,
    but occasional gliding, nurse-powered.
Motionless, but for a flapping arm, almost like a wing
    practicing flight, skin transforms to feathers.

Plumes of hair upright, but inside, an old seabird preparing
    to launch from his wheeled chariot.

Rounding skyward, an avian intervention giving sanctuary
    as his mind slides over the edge of reality.
Spending his final years airborne at sea, an escape,
    beloved birds, final companions for his voyage.

Blue Smoke
Lisa Lucas

Every day he watches them march,
their hollow steps follow a straight path
that rule out a nod,
a smile,
or him.

After school, he races to the restaurant to clean tables,
drudgery until midnight when he begs for rest.

His sleep now interrupted by feelings of loneliness that circle his head and
gain momentum to snatch the night.

Years later, the posse passes by in unison,
their steps rigid,
backs ramrod straight.

No time to search for a flicker of acknowledgement,
the restaurant consumes all,
while his mom cooks and his aunt, masked with a fake smile, serves,
he slogs until closing

Finally, late into the night, he lights a cigarette,
watches the wispy, blue-smoke rings
circle his thoughts of isolation.

Mom gone,
aunt gone,
the posse no longer in sight,
a glowing restaurant review.

Time to breathe but
with each raspy exhale,
puffs of blue-tinged rejection
fill the air.

The Barn Reapers
Susan J. Wurtzburg

Eyes focus on dust motes, yellow swirls hover,
    animal smells in the air.
Children soar between hay bales,
    excitement crackles with fear.
Voices loud, mouths wide, legs scratched,
    still, we chase and scream.
Shoes full of hay stems never slow us
    as over the bales we fly.
Games done, we empty socks and pockets
    of dried grass, brush each other off.
Clean up the youngest, glance around the barn,
    ready for departure.
Oblivious to the black-cloaked figures, scythes
    raised, who haunt our play.
Death lurks overhead; rusted bale claw held
    by a tattered rope.
Injury loiters by the open end of the barn,
    a two-floor drop into a manure pile.
Mortality dallies in the hay mows, a plunge
    to mangers or stone floors.
We are children, unaware of grim prospects
    skulking around the cows.
Back up the hill to our parents, enjoying
    cold beers in the late afternoon.
We leave the barn reapers to their dark pleasures
    as we escape the possibilities again.

Tomato Fingers
Lisa Lucas

He eyes the sweet-smelling products with delight,
pine, rainforest, lemon, and sea-blossom,
even the bleach gets a furtive glance,
although he knows to use it sparingly—for toilet bowls.

His folded rags, sponge mop, and vacuum,
have become dance partners,
always in step to make his home perfect—clean and fresh.

When his son arrives,
suppressed anger mounts,
paint starts to chip,
tomato fingers smudge,
while green mold oozes slowly from deep cracks.

Bleach in hand,
he blasts every surface,
grabs his mop tighter,
moves at breakneck speed.

Only to realize,
he can't fight the million mold spores that rain down or
the red stains forever imprinted on his furniture.

So, he surrenders,
throws down his mop and shakes the empty bottle,

Okay, dirtbag, you won!

Journey to Mitnal
Susan J. Wurtzburg

Walk into the realm of the dead,
cool caverns with ancient pot offerings.
Quartz stalactites glitter, carbide lamps
flare like fireflies, buried fifty feet
under the Maya Mountains jungle.
Twisted fissures lure us deeper.

Dripping water echoes through high caverns,
rock tears skim our skins. Moist flickers of fear,
I realize our leader lacks caving skills. Years
of bushwhacking wilderness come to the fore,
copal-scented priests murmur in my ears, no marks
of our winding course, few signals for the return.

Maya blood sacrifice, elites kept their world
secure, but I don't want to die for mine. Anxiety rides
on my back, nails grip my small pack. Novice cavers,
except for one claiming expertise. Walls whisper,
prepare a route back. No string to lay a lifeline
but my trusty bandanas, bright beacons fall behind.

The beauty of a final cavern, a ceiling hole to blue sky
high above, time to depart. I thank those wrinkled priests,
follow cotton offerings; cloth breadcrumbs lead us
through underground white stalagmite forests. Markers
in my pack, we exit the maw of the Maya underworld. Sweat
darkens my T-shirt, relief moistens my eyes, farewell Mitnal.

There Be Dragons
Susan J. Wurtzburg

Careful steps on the greasy tightrope
across the dark, seductive chasm.
Shift my eyes from the hairy monsters
who tickle my toes, lure me near.
Body floats above scaled dragons
to avoid their fetid tongues.
Sleep, a panacea for occasions
when the battle seems too hard.
Soft cotton muffles ears, eyelids
droop, body stills, mind rests.

But,

I cannot snooze away my days,
arise at dawn, a new strategy.

Rapid walk to thump seductive
demons back into dim caverns.

The breeze sustains as I greedily suck
the cool morning between my lips.
Plumeria scents, with a back note
of salty ocean, hints of green decay.
Legs fast, arms pump, lungs balloon
with effort, ribs dance to the beat.
Heart pounds out the rhythm,
blue eyes flash in the sun.
Muscles work as mind relaxes,
firm steps across the abyss for today.

Transformation
Susan J. Wurtzburg

Limbs tangle
    sweat slicks
forms of movement
    bodies fly
ballet-like battles
mostly with ourselves.

Neighbourhood dojo, haunt of awkward teens.
We rise to the occasion and to our sensei with a bow.
Years devoted to perfecting judo moves.

When travels beckon, I learn fierce self-defense.
Predators hate girls who know how to fight.
I battle many crocodiles.

Now
limbs tangle
    sweat slicks
on my terms, baby.

"We saw a raven very high above us. It called out, and the dome of the sky seemed to echo the sound. It called again and again as it flew onwards, and the mountains gave back the sound, seeming as if from their centre; a musical bell-like answering to the bird's hoarse voice."

Dorothy Wordsworth (1798) *The Alfoxden Journal*

The Howl and Silence
Lisa Lucas

I
She didn't run to comfort the baby when he cried,
the high-pitched screams would keep them safe.

> *Shut that kid up! What's wrong with him?*

She didn't respond.
Didn't need to.
The baby would tilt his head back,
produce a wolf-like howl,
a deafening weapon
to make his father's voice stop,
for the moment.

II
When the cop explained,

> *Lady, your son is disturbing the neighbours with his singing.*
> *Frankly, it's more like screeching! Haven't heard a sound like that before.*
> *We've had several complaints.*

She nodded politely and said she'd talk to him.
She didn't say a word.

III
Years later, he joined a monastery and took a vow of silence.
Told his mother he simply needed to live that way.

Ocean Alchemy
Susan J. Wurtzburg

Surface breathers, deep divers,
creators of underwater weather,
your great fins and tails stir the depths.

Currents rippled by your motions
carry deep songs and high-pitched whistles.
My ears bathed in musical water,
eyes open to the sky, I float the wavelets,
between two worlds, denizen of neither.

I drift above your mighty bulk. You cruise
the briny depths, like white clouds surf
the blue above. Abyss above and below, I drift,
eavesdrop on clicks, breathy notes, deep opera,
wish I understood whale words. Plaintive sounds,
salty echo-chamber, you cry about a gentle calf
struck by a boat off Oahu. Cetacean mother, you sing
your grief, mourning dirge echoed by Maui whales.

Sounds
Lisa Lucas

The sounds of a kitchen,
mostly predictable:
The shatter of ice when boiling water hits,
a song for tart iced tea.
The crunchy snap of an apple before the door slams,
savoured before the rush.

Sounds safely secured,

until a pot drops
onto a tile floor,
vibration jolts a memory,

adrenaline
tight

breathe.

Grave Distance
Susan J. Wurtzburg

Listen to the surface,
not understanding the depths,
dive down like a whale.

Words communicate superficially,
but without probing,
the shoals are hidden.

The unsaid found in sideways hints,
slyly hidden in covering text,
often inaccessible brail.

Without being heard,
the slippery, disquieting designs sink,
lost in oceanic midden.

Bubbles on the surface:
   we had no idea
      she never said
         if only I had known.

   Too late,
      too late.

Family Skeletons
Susan J. Wurtzburg

After an archaeology career, digging
    comes naturally to this body.
Blood and tears spilt in the past
    secure relatives' memories.
Recollections shown in facial tics,
    but challenging to regurgitate.
No morsels for offspring, secrets
    penned behind tight-pursed lips.
Mouths are not always for speaking,
    at least not in this family.
Older clan waxes determined, skeletons
    taken with them to the grave.
Cemetery visit likely in the future,
    featuring me prone on the earth.
Soil impressed by my ear, eavesdropping
    on underground conversations.
Mumbles from the deep possibly overheard,
    but unlikely, given the protagonists.

Open to the Void
Susan J. Wurtzburg

Mouth droop, drool loop, wet flow over craggy chin
down to a damp sheet, hints of other bodily sputters.
Engine failure at ninety-one, down-in-the-mouth
at the hospital ward, teeth-gape hints at the void.

Small puffs of air pass his lips, but no words break
the beeping music of emergency. Ocean of his life
scratches at the shore, still clings on to sandy grains.
Stubborn old man unwilling to depart this final bed.

Berths in ships, jeeps, and homes around the world,
a life well-lived with family by his side. Births of three
children in two cities, bearing landed immigrant status far
from his natal land. Launched himself across the ocean,
in bold albatross days. Birding glasses around his neck,
strong shanks' mare bore him forward, his herd behind.

Now, here we are. Glare of doctor's gaze, stethoscope
pressed against his ribs: bedded body, mouth open,
eyes shut. What fevered dreams play against his lids?
No speech,
    instead,
        a final gentle huff.

Beached
Susan J. Wurtzburg

Shark lightning slips on by, ominous, grey shape-shifter
for small fry in the rocks. Provokes an intake of breath
through the snorkel. My masked eyes widen as he looms
large. Expel air; this juvenile poses no threat to me. I float,
an unmoored dirigible, adrift in the current. Sun-warmed water
heats my head, drumbeat of wave surges in my ears,
adrenaline-fueled elation, perfect morning in the Pacific.

Turtle scrapes a beaked mouth across algal beds, legs churn,
energetic pistons that drive him onward. Out in the bay,
I hear the echoing moans of humpbacks, migratory
visitors celebrating Hawaii with their young. Songs ring
in my ears as I crawl from the ocean, primeval being
moving up the sand. Hands on knees, bent before covid rates
and risks, beached on a rock in the middle of the Pacific.

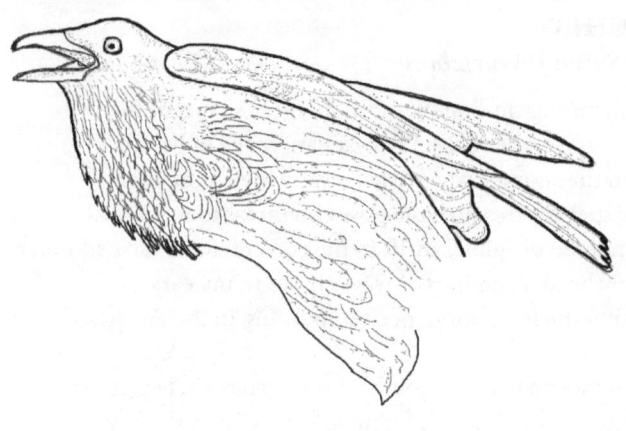

"He flies for the joy of flying,
He lights for the moment's whim,
And when he is ready for dying
The earth approves of him."

Virginia Moore (1928) "Justified Bird"

Old Monk
Lisa Lucas

Fur thins, teeth rot, breath reeks, blind and deaf,

supposedly 133 in human years and still eats well,

loves,

walks,

no, mainly stumbles.

But always expending his energy like an Olympian,
with precision,
steady and sure.

A friend calls him an old monk,
full of purpose,
knowing exactly what to do to stay alive,
seemingly enlightened,
seemingly free.

My Friend Said
Susan J. Wurtzburg

"La vida es como un pañuelo,"
we circuit the school track.
I laugh, puzzled by the phrase,
foreign to my ears, in Yucatán.
She removes her bandana,
pulls the corners together,
creates red-cloth arch.

Two women meet in Mérida,
México, each far from home.
Last together in the USA.
What are the odds?
Perhaps the world folds,
a handkerchief, and we
balance on its crease.

Winter Light
Lisa Lucas

I

Trudge through the new snow,
peer through the windows,
hard to distinguish
until a ray of light sparks imagination.

Is that a bare bum?
A velvet rose?
An O'Keefe-inspired azalea?

Walk a few steps closer and spot an enormous canvas,
an exquisite flower emerges smack in the middle.

Lights suddenly turn off,
darkness engulfs the petals,
gentle laughs are muffled and awaken joy.

II

Tired eyes blink at the thousands of bright lights that scream out,

Aren't I spectacular! Look at my colours! Look at me pulse!

Dare to look away and a blinding flash,

Don't turn your head! Look at ME! ME! ME!
White! Green and Red!

Cold hands reach out and clasp fingers,
an escape ensues through the grey snow and the jagged ice
until the pulsing lights fade and blurred vision forces eyes to shut.

Midnight Stallions
Susan J. Wurtzburg

Some nights, I summon a black horse,
whose back I mount at midnight,
and I fly away from here.

Pegasus throws sparks from his hooves,
gallops me through the streets. Pass
my neighbours' dim-lit homes, leap
the beach barricade. Run the strand
to exhaustion, collapse in the sand.

No stallions for English girls, years ago,
but bicycles. Three night-gowned youngsters
mount their metal steeds, roam ghost-like
in the gloaming. Stealth-climb the wall,
second-floor window, sneak back to bed.
Under cotton sheets, plots for the morrow,
exploration, an ongoing theme. But now,

no real adventures, instead confined to dreams.

"Under wide driven wings of cloud, and under
The unseen heavy-beating wings of thunder
   Are wings of birds,
Now tossed like blowing leaves on a windy plain,
Now held suspended a moment, immobile; again
   Like a rush of words …"

                Glenn Ward Dresbach (1928) "Birds in the Wind"

Daffodils
Susan J. Wurtzburg

A shell of a man, not as pretty as the phrase.
Rather than a pearlescent, rosy nautilus,
instead a bombed-out brain. Bleary eyesight
like the mollusk, blue eyes track movement uneasily.

Murmured caring tones mere noise
to his ears. Few words emitted through chapped lips,
mostly, "No." His clock has lost its
winding mechanism, with a reset to basic wants.

One hand hard-clamped on bed railing, the other
limply rests. No muscle strength for a signature,
let alone the mental will. This present weakness
never envisioned by the younger man.

Yellow-taloned feet, lizard-like appendages, a dry
desert of skin needs lotion. Angry arms wave,
drowning in his bed, hisses, "Leave me alone."
Parent without memory of caring for the child.

Loving touch, vision, words fail miserably.
Little remains within his carapace.

Then I read the Wordsworth title, "I wandered lonely as a cloud."

This gaunt man mutters, "Daffodils."

Here's the Thing ...
Lisa Lucas

She loved hopscotch.
She'd jump from square to square
without a misstep
or line touched.

With every jump,
she'd laugh,
telling her friends
that she was right
'cause she knew her thoughts counted
and her judgment
was spot on.

Yes!
She won the game.
Every single game.
Jumping perfectly
into those ten squares.

When friends questioned
a thought,
an assumption,
she jumped
more precisely,
more accurately,
all the while repeating,

Here's the thing...
Here's the thing...

And over time,
playing hopscotch was no longer fun
for her friends,
so they stopped playing
while she jumped
and jumped
from square to square
without a misstep
or line touched.

We Call This Land
Susan J. Wurtzburg

Our southern lowland soils break on the granite of the Canadian Shield.
Stones and glacial dust flow to open water along the Abitibi, Missinaibi,
Ekwan, Mikwam, Lawashi, Kabika, Wapesi, Mattagami, and Kesagami.
We call our homes: Winisk, Wawa, Petawawa, Penetanguishene,
Atikokan, Kenora, Kapuskasing, Temiskaming, Temagami, and Toronto.

Our days marked by Timmie's donuts, butter tarts, maple
syrup, while wearing mukluks, toques, and jackets. We work
in urban settings, still know our farmers, foresters, trappers.
Road and rail connected, but in the north, Cessna with a canoe
strapped to a float, and fishing line on board, the way to travel.

Winters huddled in cities, summer escapes to sunny lakes,
a thousand miles north to south, about the same east to west,
all of it mapped. Oblivious to theodolites and surveying rods;
beaver, moose, and deer roam their lands. Range established
with dams, scat, and tracks, no further ownership claimed.

The Damn Page
Lisa Lucas

Stare,
hope,
a page—white, blank, boundless,
waits
for a thought
a story
a new life.

Out of nowhere,
well—probably somewhere,
a rough idea pops,
a protagonist pops,
a storyline pops,
a name pops
        pops
                pops

Penelopop—a perfect name for a new beginning.

Her music will be her superpower.
She'll master the ukulele, the drums, the trumpet.
Her music will save her friends from a nasty villain
who shrivels at the striking sounds she creates.
Is she imperfect? —yes. Interesting? —yes. Clever? —very,
and all wrapped up in 426 words.

Kids will love it!

Time for the publishers, editors, agents
to examine the newborn,
to discuss her worthiness.

Months pass and Penelopop returns,
assessed.

> *Well, it's certainly unique alright.*
> *The character,*
> *the story,*
> *nothing like it out there.*
> *Well done!*

> *We want it.*
> *But there is one thing.*
> *The name.*
> *Can you call her Susan?*

Don't respond,
    can't respond.

Stare at another page—white, blank, boundless,
an endless search
until a boy appears.
He's tiny.
He needs to find a loud voice to save the trees,
but the king tries to stop him until his tiny voice gets louder and stronger
with the help of a gigantic megaphone and . . .

Yes—it works.
A character—almost insignificant, who saves the environment,
and in only 392 words.

Kids will love it!

Time for the publishers, editors, agents.
Tiny returns in record time.

> *Hmmm . . . leave it to you!*
> *It's certainly unique.*
> *The tiny character with the huge voice.*
> *Good juxtaposition.*
> *Interesting.*
> *Well done!*
> *We'll take it.*
> *But—the king.*
> *Shouldn't it be a president?*
> *After all, kids need to learn the electoral system.*

Don't respond,
    can't respond.

The damn page is back.

A Very British War
Susan J. Wurtzburg

Green-bound annuals rest on a table in my office,
    labelled 1907-1917.
A familial Rosetta stone, my great-grandmother's
    penned impressions.
Her calligraphy saunters up and down pages,
    sometimes circles itself,
    an investigative challenge.

Like a linguist deciphering ancient texts,
    I follow her cursive route.
Hieroglyphic tales of walks, church
    attendance, and a world war.
A cartouche of my grandmother's twentieth
    birthday, and her hospital work
    with battle-scarred men.

Icons of troop movements and billets, interspersed
    with family news.
Stolen moments in the village, tamped-down worry
    about serving sons and brothers.
A whole generation of family killed in battle,
    determinatives between the diary's script,
    buried in lighter news of afternoon tea.

Bumper Cars and Rockets
Lisa Lucas

She gasped at the sight of the bumper cars. Especially the steel pole mounted at the back: the conduit for the electric current to jolt the small metal vehicles forward and slam others from behind.

Ahhh! Don't be chicken!

Her best friend screamed and pointed to the last empty one in the corner.

Hurry up!
Jump in!

Her mother scrambled to glue thick rubber padding to the sides,
but the car took off,
left the bare metal to buckle with every bump,
the impact seen through the scratched paint.

For years, she avoided all forms of transportation.

Until much to everyone's surprise, she climbed into a rocket, fastened herself tightly, and blasted off. When she reached space, she fell in love with the sensation of weightlessness in her muscles and bones.

And there she rested with no bumps or bruises.

Until far out in space,
a figure approached,
he moved straight ahead,
directly towards her,
nothing to take him off course,
nothing to change.

And in space, they lived quietly together,
in slow, uniform motion,
with no friction or force,
until they knew it was time
to return to earth.

Quilted Heritage
Susan J. Wurtzburg

Old patched quilts hang over a ladder in a sun-filled corner of the bedroom.
The most colourful one, perhaps a hundred years old, surprisingly intact.
Its white background interspersed with patterned fabric vibrantly abloom,
delicately repaired by my grandmother, whose tiny stitches can be tracked.
Sewn by hand, a dying skill, women gifting their eyesight to a family's warmth.
These heavy cotton quilts map the genealogy of relationships up north.

These ragged family coverlets, now imported to Hawaii, renowned for the shaka.
My northern heritage fits surprisingly well, given the importance of *kapa kuiki*.
Women's sewing skills overlaid on the historic production of bark cloth *tapa*,
honoured in the islands, since even royalty made quilts, unlikely to disappear.
Place of new and old combined, layered meanings, this golden-sanded island
offers a home to my cobbled-together self and cotton-recorded genealogy.

Loot, Bookmarks, and The J Stroke
Lisa Lucas

I
Her sisters-in-law watched in awe:
> *Now that's a show!*
> *A real Olympic performance.*
> *She might even win the gold for competitive grieving.*

The puffy gold jacket glistened as she draped herself over the dead body,
her loud cries,
now a cacophony of minor notes,
performance art for the old man she despised,
choreographed to grab his loot.

II
A coffee date with her oldest friend,
a chance to speak of her mother:
> *Her sewing kit was full of bookmarks.*
> *You know, I had no idea she made them.*
> *Here's one for you.*
> *She'd want you to have it.*

Antique buttons anchored a blue silk ribbon at both ends,
a quiet symbol, beautifully crafted
to mark her place.

III
They travelled far to be at her side,
shared memories sandwiched between liquid meals, medication, and bedpans,
laughs often heard from the warm, home-like atmosphere of the hospice room.
When family and jobs demanded two of them resume their lives,
they urged the youngest:
> *Mom could last for months.*
> *Don't hold vigil.*
> *She wouldn't want that.*
> *Take those canoe lessons she bought you.*

The mother passed as she wanted,
alone,
while her baby practiced the J stroke with a blue single-bladed paddle.

Departures
Susan J. Wurtzburg

Farmhouse morning, skunk scent swirls
in the window. Black-and-white odour
sour on my tongue complemented
by loon songs. Red squirrels chitter
among green walnuts, chase tails,
energy soars with the rising sun.

Gilded globe vaporizes dewy droplets,
warm rivulets flow down the hill.
Water twirls, warbler stirs with his beak
as he prepares for the autumn migration.

"We need a fire," Mum says,
as she glances into the airy bedroom.
White-haired, old pants, striped shirt,
ready for another golden-streaked day.

Fifty years unspool: I see a broad smile,
my younger mother glides the corridor,
pristine floorboards, white painted hall.

Today: walls baggage-scarred,
floors scraped by dashing shoes,
as family hurries out the door.

In the Mountains
Susan J. Wurtzburg

Just an ordinary day in the Andes, youthful
    archaeologists focus on the past.
El terrorismo de Sendero Luminoso

1982, ignoring politics, we map and excavate
    ancient features, Northern Peru.
un grupo militar y político.

On that evening, we bring the equipment downhill,
    joyful in the mountain sun.
Las dos décadas de terrorismo

My shoulder weighted by a surveying tripod,
    smooth metal pinches.
entre 1980 y el 2000.

The fastest route to town, not the local trails,
    but a direct transect.
Campesinos brutalmente asesinados

Back in the square, military visitors label us
    "Sendero Luminoso," plot death.
lucha contra la gente.

Locals know the project, save our lives. No
    rescue for Quechua boys two days later.
Tres campesinos murieron.

INSIDE
Lisa Lucas

Inside this brown bag is a soapstone,
a small carving,
a grey and white structure,
shiny and smooth,
rocks piled on top of one another,
an Inukshuk,
a land marker,
a beacon,
for the way home.

> *Here she goes.*
> *Nana being Nana.*
> *Sounds all wise 'n all.*
> *As if I care about a bunch of dumb rocks.*

A form that reveals journeys,
when folklore has been used up
and there are no words left to describe the challenges you've faced.

> *She's at it again.*
> *Yes, yes, that time was hard—my absolute rock bottom,*
> *but this stone isn't going to do a damn thing to help.*
> *Nana, please drop it.*

I know your road has been long,
barriers obstructed your path,
deceit took you the long way,
often winding you round,
'til you dropped from exhaustion.

> *She just can't seem to stop herself today.*
> *Weird, she rarely goes on and on like this.*
> *Something's up.*

Hold it,
really touch it,
'cause I know the smooth stone will be there
for the journeys you've already navigated,
and the ones to come.

Okay, okay, I'll touch it if it pleases you, old lady.
Yah, it is crazy smooth.
A Mac truck couldn't pull this thing apart.
What's it called?
An Inuk-a-tuk?

                                        I guess I'll put it beside my bed.
                                        Nah, in my pocket.

"What are these ravens doing in our trees,
Calling on doom and outworn prophecies?"

> Louis Untermeyer (1928) "Business of Ravens"

A Louisiana Rabbit
Susan J. Wurtzburg

Scruffy backwoods archaeology,
    metal tools in my red truck.
Stock a little disreputable, duct-tape
    repairs, metal-hanger aerial.
Post-hurricane retools add panache
    to this rusty, extended-cab Toyota.

A householder points in the direction,
    a short drive to the cemetery.
In my rear mirror, a truck follows, driven
    by the helpful, now-scary man.
I run from the pickup, glimpse his gun,
    recoil groundward to shiver.

Elusive rabbit, I endure, not sure what he wants,
    not interested in his trigger.
Old weapon scars my truck, but no hammer
    pulls, and he shoots home.
A rapid departure, my safe option. No police
    call made. After all, this is Louisiana.

Caste Wars
Lisa Lucas

The bright yellow light blinked,
an exclamation mark
surrounded by what looked like a cross-section of a tire.
The rear right was vibrating.

When she opened the door and saw Pussface,
an unlit cigarette pasted to his bottom lip,
a gas smell emanating from his body,
her shoulders seized.

She tightened the metal strip at the top of her mask,
well aware she'd need her virus armour
and explained why she was there.

Her years of executive training made her good at that:

> **Always make three points to get the information across.**
> **Make them short and emphasize the first and last.**

She figured that way, even this moron could understand.

> *Barely heard what you just said under that thing, little lady.*
> *You wanna try again, or should I tell you the kinda troubles you got.*

Pussface kicked the right rear.

> *You see this here?*
> *They call it a run flat.*
> *Piece of shit as far as I'm concerned.*
> *They use them on fancy cars like yours.*
> *They say you can drive miles on these after a puncture.*
> *Joke is no one really knows.*
> *You could have been shit outta luck.*
> *Stranded.*
> *Just ripe for the picking.*

He burst out laughing and pointed his yellow-stained finger.

> *You see that Ford over there,*

> *2012 and don't it look nice?*
> *289K and still running just fine.*
> *It's seen a few things in that there back seat—but ain't right for your ears.*
> *Now, I just bet you'll never guess;*
> *my tires cost a fraction of what you've got here on your chariot.*

He lit the hanging cigarette and snickered,

> *So, what do you wanna do, pretty lady?*
> *Don't have all day.*
> *You want me to replace that rear right of yours?*

She rearranged her mask for full coverage,
yanked her designer bag closer and grinned,

> *Yes, replace it.*
>
> > *No! Replace all four.*

Almost Airborne
Susan J. Wurtzburg

Women resemble albatrosses:

Both linked   to misfortune

     by   men's tales.

I feel my back   for wing stubs

   —none present   yet

but might they   still erupt?

     Soft feathers of down

       to pluck from my breast

         a velvety pillow of my body.

A long imperious beak

   to squawk indignation noisily   while still not being heard.

      Endangered   by men

       and sadly,   also women.

       When   will my body morph

        to that   of bird?

       I am ready   to fly far

      from this burnt-out wasteland.

Image: Flaticon.com

His Mother's Words
Lisa Lucas

Probably narcissism,
the disorder—hard to treat, hard to break—infiltrated his life at fourteen.

When the Germans occupied his world,
when he almost starved,
when his mother offered little but praise.

You are perfect!
Do you hear me? Perfect!
He was told . . . and told.

Didn't matter that he was average at everything,
'cause she'd find another way for his success,
teach him a work ethic, a discipline.

Get him up early to tidy his room,
exercise,
    finish his homework,
        practice the piano,
            go to school,
                do more homework,
                      eat dinner,
                            go to bed,
                                and repeat.

Until one small triumph after another
morphed into pistons transferring his incremental strength into narcissism
and grandiosity whispered in his ear,
Yup, you really are perfect.

And sure enough, he was able to get A's and B's,
an engineering degree,
a good job.

He found a bride and told her,
What do you know? I know, you don't!
And soon, she believed it.

Eventually, worthlessness killed her,

his daughters ran away,
his eldest son broke,
all while he listened attentively to his mother's words.

Identity Bracelets
Susan J. Wurtzburg

At age thirteen, I receive a chain-link bracelet,
name engraved. Flaunt my gift, never consider
my body, now identified. Groups of girls on the subway,
self-referential plaques bound over bony wrists. Bright coils
connect them to families for perpetuity, a leashed present.

At that time, the news features Vietnam,
but we live north, beyond war casualties.

Unaware that dog tags circle necks of American troops,
children eye friends and grades. Sliding bracelets up our arms,
we fail to imagine Southern mothers' tears on sons' tags. Naively,
no thought that trips to work or school might be our final experiences.

Now, exposed to bloodshot violence growling across the USA,
I envision little girls already labelled for the cold, dark burial ground.

Self Portrait
Lisa Lucas

Private schools, camps, holidays, horses, museums, galleries, and
a mother nudging him towards the arts.

So, he listened and studied
line, colour, texture,
all the masters.

With time, his mother's wishes took shape and slowly morphed into
sailboats, horses, dogs, and memories of travel.

All carefully imagined.
All carefully crafted.

Until an art critic wrote,

Art imprisoned by privilege . . .
unconsciously executed.

Travels with My Brother
Susan J. Wurtzburg

"Whatever you do, don't take your brother to Guatemala,"
    so we crossed from Belize to Mexico.
My brother: taller than age fifteen, with me, his responsible adult,
    only twenty-two, but a seasoned solo-traveler.
Guided on jungle adventures by an internalized rainforest wolf:
    strong muscles, quick responses, solitary.

Careful anti-theft precautions: paper next to skin, under clothing; soggy bills
    heat our chests, waists, and feet.
Money and passports hidden, we feel secure, grin at each other, joke
    our way across towns and borders.
We stroll Mérida streets, bus station-based simple room, sibling adventurers
    amidst Mexican travelers.

Roll the roads to Uxmal, explore structures built by ancient Maya architects,
    climb steps trod by past elite.
My wolfish alter ego guides us through the brush to outlying structures,
    less frequented portions of the site.
Charles battles vertigo at temple tops, but follows boldly. At the summits,
    peer in all directions, avoid snakes.

Our hiking boots firmly plant themselves on stone. My brother's shorts,
    my modest sundress with T-shirt, functional wardrobes.
Canines don't care about appearance, withstand the elements in heavy fur,
    strong legs rest on thick paw pads, impervious to thorns.
This wolf's companion, my brother, laughs at my anecdotes, tracks my lead,
    while his presence keeps me safe.

When Mexico Belly strikes, he is down for the count. I hit the road,
    in search of pharmaceutical aid.
Confidence about fighting skills, along with fast-running legs,
    maintains my wild self-assurance.

Composure thrown to the pavement.
    Dress pulled waist high.
        Fingers trail my body.
            People avert their eyes.
                Furious, I punch their sons.
                    They laugh, undaunted.

                I bare my teeth.
                Holler "hijos de puta."

Receive disapproval from elders along the thoroughfare,
    who shake their heads: a rabbit attacked by curs,
    who savage, but don't bite in a desultory type of fight.

Disheveled on the sidewalk, I lick my wounds,
    brush down my wolfish hair, arrange my dress,
    and stride forward, with flashing golden eyes.

THE ATTRACTION OF GRIEF
Lisa Lucas

He named it *Sad Ball*.

Starting off no bigger than a marble rolling around. He could handle that.

Weeks trudged by and *Sad Ball* got bigger, growing into a tennis ball, a beach ball, eventually morphing into a large circular sphere.

Unable to resist the attraction of immense grief,
Sad Ball gained speed and barreled towards him.

And through tears, he touched it,

    and held it frighteningly close,

        and with time it shrank.

            but not completely.

(For J.B.)

If You Can
May, 2020
Lisa Lucas

Socially distance
Wash your hands
Wear a mask
Stay at home

For the privileged, it will be time to try new things—rest, read, cocoon, Zoom with friends, or bake sourdough. Yup, there's a recipe circulating online for a great starter.

And for the control freaks, it will probably be hell cause that spiky devil is unpredictable and can latch onto anything. Yes, that could be you! So, you'll need to work real hard—to control racing thoughts, to meditate, to exercise. You can download some apps for that.

Now for the health-care workers and those who have no choice but to be out there, try to breathe—one breath at a time. Then put a foot down, then the next. Keep going. Try to recognize your strength with every minute and hour that passes. You know, if you're lucky, by the end of the day, you'll have a sliver of energy to face the next.

But let's be real. All your thoughts and effort will probably get worn down and merge into an explosion of anxiety and sadness. A loud, deafening BOOM! And all that will matter, will be to get through . . .

        if you can.

I've Seen Everything
Case # 08-28
Lisa Lucas

You see that judge up there?
I have to stand beside the jerk almost every day
in case some whack-a-doodle gets too close.

Look at him in those dumb black robes,
nose in the air,
convinced he's the smartest in the room,
Mr. Brilliant Head.

Now take those docs that fix the mushy grey stuff in our brains,
and give a lucky bugger a second chance,
or them teachers at those fancy schools that speak like ten languages.
Say "a ruk tik tuk" and they get it. They know what it means.
Makes kids feel good about themselves,
like their words count.

Now, that's smart!
Let me tell you, this guy ain't that.

Just last month, a young fella walked in,
kind of light-in-the-foot if you know what I mean,
came all the way from a place I think called Masadooneo.

Story goes that he had to get out in a hurry,
playing on the other team and all.

There he stood, shaking in his boots
when the prick decided to make one of his big scenes.

Get up and give me your phone!
So, are you really gay?
You do understand that if I let you stay, you're going to cost this country a helluva
    lot of money.
Now let's take a look at what we have here.
Oh ya, sure looks like it.
Do you have a dating account? Forget it, I got it.
Oh ya ...

The fucker stared at the screen for way too long,
probs got a few kicks.
Finally handed it to me to give back to the poor sucker.
Good thing he was seated by then 'cause he sure did look sick.

I heard that the guy got to stay.
But you know, for a long time I felt real bad for him and
I've seen everything.

(For Tommy)

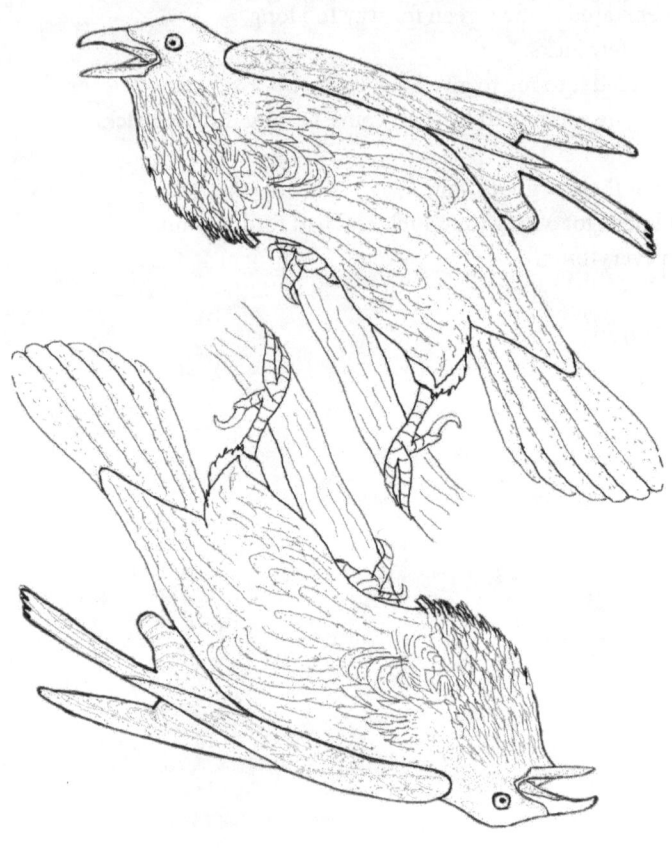

"O sweet and luminous Bird,
Having once heard Your call, lovely and shy,
I shall be hungry for the finished word."

Jessica Powers (1928) "Celestial Bird"

My Sister
Susan J. Wurtzburg

My sister enacts meal provider, her people cluster
    around the table.
Sustenance for empty bodies and hearts, hollowed
    out by this year.

I am far—across the Pacific Ocean,
    fed by my family.
In the midst of food plenty, hungry,
    lonely days here.

Rib-shielded, the emptiness lessened
    by video calls.
Threads across the waves from my island
    to her wooded home.

My sibling draws me back to Canada, distant
    pines and lakes.
Each call a step closer. Yet still stranded
    on a rock
        in the ocean.

Two Meals
Lisa Lucas

I
He smiles at the plate placed before him
before he rips the flesh off the bones and gnaws
only to break for a slurp of beer that runs down his beard
and knots the hair with barley and hops into a tangled web.

Noxious, jumbled sounds of animal muscle, globules of fat and cold liquid
carry the mélange down and with each throaty contraction,
wet gurgling becomes audible.

I turn away until words barrel out . . .

thoughtful, precise, and hopeful words,

a prayer of sorts.

II
She eyes the chicken breast with precision,
turns her fork down,
picks up her knife and begins to cut methodically,
back and forth, to produce small, rectangular bites,
impossible for her to be caught with a full mouth.

A small sip of chardonnay gently bathes the animal's flesh and
a quiet gulp pushes it down.

She smiles at me with wide eyes.
I smile back.

She takes an inaudible breath and in a melodious voice sings . . .

vicious, savage, and spiteful words,

a camouflaged rant.

Narnia Notions
Susan J. Wurtzburg

No lions appear as I open the wardrobe door;

instead, many versions of me droop limply,
waiting for opportunity. Warm sweaters,
homes for moths as I pause family visits.
Hiking shoes neglected, multi-day explorations
postponed. Sleeping bag curls dejectedly,
no camping in my future. Ski jacket puffs on a hanger,
fluffy down sighs. Bright dresses await a party,
a chance to perform. Well-used shorts, casual T-shirts
slink out the closet door quietly, avoid jealousy
of other clothes. Leisure garb for uncomfortable times.

Distress registered through clothing, but no lions
peering between hangers or clawing at my arms.
Fingers click the wardrobe door shut. I know my luck;
no need this past year for dark, funeral clothes.

Her North Star
Lisa Lucas

At three, little interaction with her dolls;
rather, a discerning examination
of the soft fabric flowing down the small plastic hips,
fastened by two ivory buttons and thread.

She cinches the waist with the white silk ribbon
intended for her hair.
She knows this is where it really belongs.

Oblivious to the pull of her star,
her self-determination
is being seeded.

> At eleven, she rams letters together
> to form a quagmire of words and sentences.
>
> Frustrated by the jumbled imperfection,
> she quickly learns to avoid the classroom.
> Only night stars settle her thoughts.
>
> At forty-one, a barrage of nasty words,
> and flying fists,
> force her to drop the pretense.
>
> And in her aloneness,
> she inches forward towards the light.

(For Christine S.)

Pandemic Journeys
Susan J. Wurtzburg

A rather boring grocery list clutched in my hand,
I venture into Safeway. A good name for this current
time of trouble, although it doesn't always feel safe,
as such. Blueberries, bananas, oh yes, some apples,
since we are trying to eat healthily to stave off illness.

Aisles are directional, which still seems challenging for some,
not sure why this is so difficult. Masked figures stomp
boldly toward me, making me feel less than friendly.
Milk, beer, and orange juice placed in the cart, a few treats
are needed at home. Simple pleasures in hard times.

Not everyone understands Hawaii health directives,
although all wear facial coverings in the store.
One day, the words "fuckhead" escaped my lips, but
that guy pushed by me. Mostly, I am polite, trying
to model appropriate aloha. Oh, yes, I need chocolate.

I feel more nervous in Safeway than during any lone jungle
expedition. Walking around verdant Corcovado,
Costa Rica, in 1982, was far less nerve-racking.
Yes, I braved thirst, sharks, and alligators, but careless
young men are my new fear. Yup, wine is on the list.

Her Spirit Animal
Lisa Lucas

Her Spirit Animal leads her to writing.

Always there, always hiding,
the hunt continues.

Cardinals seem to look her way,
almost stare.
She hopes their wings will make their way inside and flutter
to lift a story,
    a poem,
        a few words onto a page.

But stillness endures.

Until one clear night,
when the stars, the moon, and silver rays take form,
it comes,
clearly,
without doubt,

her Spirit Animal.

Eating the Rainbow
Susan J. Wurtzburg

The morning fades to green,
she feels its colour on her tongue,
that rusty note with rotten tones.
Green again. She cannot stand
another stinging-nettle day.

In times of old, a shaman,
but here today, neurodiverse,
senses scrambled. No renown
or respect, invisible disability,
scarlet D on her back.

It is a small village.

Jacket in hand, hat on head,
she staggers down the hill,
visits the cobble-filled shore
again. This time, she rounds
her pockets with ashen stones.

Dull grey, colour of desolation,
grief, and despair. Combined
with green, weighs too much.
Grey tastes dusty, slate-like
bitterness of her youth.

She wades into murky, tan water,
shoulders bowed. Brown dirt
on her tongue, silty, granular
between her teeth. The grit
of living in dust-blown times.

Shoeless, a few steps to the depths,
taste of colours topples her downward.
Lightning flash on the horizon sparks
sweetness in her mouth, mother's milk,
her final sensory stutter, synapses static.

Rectangular Treasure
Lisa Lucas

My bar of soap sat untouched while I waited for something special,
so I could smell like pine—pure like nature.

When the news raged and the media buzzed,
I ripped off the green wrapping, squeezed the rectangular treasure until my
fingerprints were deeply imprinted and pitched it into a steaming bath.

For when my youngest called,
frantic about her boss who berated her every move,
seemingly unaware of his tirade.

Or when I thought of my eldest on nights,
covid raging,
panicked and scared,
the fingerprints faded until the soap was smooth,
flawless as it shrank.

The soap was for then.

For the sorrows of my daughters,
the injustice of George Floyd,
the handcuffs slapped on Omar Jimenez,
the tragedy of Kobe Bryant . . .

My shrinking soap, a grateful respite,
so I could smell like pine—pure like nature.

Sweet with a Dash of Salt
Susan J. Wurtzburg

Mandarin oranges, taste of summer,
delightful weight on my palm. I feed
my grocery cart. Golden globes rest
on metal ribs, promise better days,
glow of sunny hours with friends.

Companions peel fruit with me,
scatter white salt on the segments,
pop luscious pieces in our mouths.
Tart juice bursts on our tongues,
tears flavour our eating pleasure.

No delight for the harvesters
of our gilded bounty. Men, women,
teens pluck fruit in hot Florida. Brown
fingers reach high in the trees, bodies
drip sweat, gain insufficient gold.

Maya workers battle Sunshine State
for human rights. Salt-drenched pickers
sleep interrupted by neighbours' cries,
aches and fevers untreated, risk so much
for our salted sweet-mandarin day.

Disconnected
Lisa Lucas

She asked her kids over for baked mac 'n cheese every week,
an anchor she needed after he checked out.

She grabbed a cookbook that opened to reveal orange-stained instructions,
now barely visible,
a constant that steadied her through the ongoing turbulence.

Tonight, the recipe would have to wait.
She needed an oven that worked—one that didn't sputter or lose heat.

She'd have to order in,
a call she knew would bring the old workhorse
closer to being obsolete for the first time in thirty-three years.

The next week, its gas line was disconnected, and the movers hauled it away.
She turned her head when the old man wheezed,
Ta, never seen one of these hang on this long,
as he struggled with his hacksaw to cut the last inch of pipe, sweat pooling on his brow.

When the two burly workers, mumbling under their breath, lifted the pieces of metal onto the dolly and plonked it at the end of the driveway, she slipped into her bedroom.
Through the window, she stared at the bent hinges and burners,
an unceremonious burial ground for the ravens
to pick through the remnants of the thousands of meals that
comforted, celebrated, and nourished.

Credits

Thanks to the editors of the following journals in which some of these poems first appeared, sometimes in slightly different versions or with different titles.

Better than Starbucks: "My Friend Said"
Crab Creek Review: "In the Mountains"
Crosswinds: "Out of the Box in the USA"
The Fictional Café: "My Sister"
Hawaii Pacific Review: "Quilted Heritage"
The Literary Nest: "The Barn Reapers" (republished in *Sanctuary Magazine*)
Love in the Time of Covid: A Chronicle of a Pandemic: "Sliding over the Edge" and "Sounds"
The Pen Woman: "Almost Airborne"
Quail Bell Magazine: "Inside," "Loot, Bookmarks and The J Stroke" and "Pink Steel Rocket"
Rat's Ass Review: "Transformation," "A Very British War" and "Pandemic Journeys"
Spillwords: "I've Seen Everything (Case #08-28)" and "Old Mirror"
Verse-Virtual: "Daffodils"

"In the Mountains" semifinalist in the *Crab Creek Review* Poetry Competition, 2022.
"Sweet with a Dash of Salt" awarded 1st place in the Elizabeth M. Campbell Poetry Award, organized by the National League of American Pen Women, 2022.

About the Authors

Susan J. Wurtzburg retired from an academic career at the University of Hawaii at Manoa, and now lives in Salt Lake City, Utah. Her poetry is grounded in the USA and Canada, where she was born, with some pieces set in Central and South America, where she worked as an archaeologist. In addition to sense of place, her literary output focuses on gender, ethnicity, and the environment. Wurtzburg received 1st place in the Land of Enchantment Award, and the Save Our Earth Award (National Federation of State Poetry Societies), 2024; as well as the Elizabeth M. Campbell Poetry Award (National League of American Pen Women), 2022. She was a semi-finalist in the *Crab Creek Review* Poetry Competition 2022, and in the *Naugatuck River Review*'s 14th Narrative Poetry Contest, 2022. Wurtzburg was a Community Poet in the Spring 2023 Poetry Workshop, Westminster College, Salt Lake City. She is a Commissioned Artist in *Sidewalk Poetry: Senses of Salt Lake City*, 2024; and serves as an Associate Poetry Editor with *Poets Reading the News*. www.susanwurtzburg.com.

Lisa Lucas began her career writing for magazines and newspapers. Later, she wrote extensively on issues related to literacy and health that were featured in publications by the Canadian Public Health Association, several literacy organizations, and hospitals across Canada. She is the recipient of the CIBC Children's Miracle Maker Award for advancing literacy among people with special needs. Several years ago, Lisa partnered with Laurie Stein, an illustrator, and began writing for children covering subjects from climate change to refugees. Their work has been recognized by *The New York Times*, *Kirkus Reviews* (starred), *Publishers Weekly*, and more. Their books have been translated into several languages and are widely recognized throughout Canada and the US. More recently, Lisa has turned her attention to poetry and historical fiction. She has had the privilege of collaborating with John Kapelos, Steve Landsberg, Balaji Swaminath, and of course Susan Wurtzburg on this anthology. lisalucas.ca

www.ingramcontent.com/pod-product-compliance
Lightning Source LLC
LaVergne TN
LVHW011428080426
835512LV00005B/331